Anonymous

Vespers of the Blessed Virgin

And Benediction of the Blessed Sacrament in Latin and English

Anonymous

Vespers of the Blessed Virgin
And Benediction of the Blessed Sacrament in Latin and English

ISBN/EAN: 9783337331283

Printed in Europe, USA, Canada, Australia, Japan

Cover: Foto ©Thomas Meinert / pixelio.de

More available books at **www.hansebooks.com**

VESPERS

OF THE

BLESSED VIRGIN,

AND

BENEDICTION

OF THE

BLESSED SACRAMENT,

in Latin and English.

WITH SUITABLE HYMNS.

LONDON:

THOMAS RICHARDSON AND SON;

DUBLIN, AND DERBY.

1871.

VESPERÆ DE B. MARIA VIRGINE.

Pater Noster et Ave Maria, Secreto.

V. Deus in adjutorium meum intende.

R. Domine ad adjuvandum me festina.

Gloria Patri, et Filio, * et Spiritui Sancto.

Sicut erat in principio, et nunc, et semper, * et in sæcula sæculorum. Amen. Alleluia.

Vel, Laus tibi Domine, Rex æternæ gloriæ.

Ant. Dum esset Rex in accubitu suo, nardus mea dedit odorem suavitatis.

Psalmus 109.

Dixit Dominus Domino meo : * Sede a dextris meis :

Donec ponam inimicos tuos, * scabellum pedum tuorum.

Virgam virtutis tuæ emittet Dominus ex Sion : * dominare in medio inimicorum tuorum.

Tecum principium in die virtutis tuæ in splendoribus sanctorum : * ex utero ante luciferum genui te.

VESPERS OF THE B. VIRGIN.

The Our Father and Hail Mary being said in silence, the Priest sings aloud,

V. O God, come to my assistance.

R. O Lord, make haste to help me.

Glory be to the Father, and to the Son, and to the Holy Ghost.

As it was in the beginning, is now, and ever shall be, world without end. Amen. Alleluia.

Or, Praise be to Thee, O Lord, King of eternal glory.

Ant. While the King was on his couch, my spikenard yielded a sweet odour.

Psalm 109.

The Lord said to my Lord : Sit thou at my right-hand :

Until I make thine enemies thy footstool.

The Lord will send forth the sceptre of thy power out of Sion : rule thou in the midst of thine enemies.

With thee is the principality in the day of thy strength, in the brightness of the saints : from the womb, before the daystar, I begot thee.

Juravit Dominus, et non pœnitebit eum : * Tu es sacerdos in æternum secundum ordinem Melchisedech.

Dominus a dextris tuis, * confregit in die iræ suæ reges.

Judicabit in nationibus, implebit ruinas : * conquassabit capita in terra multorum.

De torrente in via bibet : * propterea exaltabit caput.

Gloria Patri, et Filio, * et Spiritui Sancto.

Sicut erat in principio, et nunc, et semper, * et in sæcula sæculorum. *Amen.*

Ant. Dum esset Rex in accubitu suo, nardus mea dedit odorem suavitatis.

Ant. Læva ejus sub capite meo, et dextera illius amplexabitur me.

Psalmus 112.

Laudate, pueri, Dominum : * laudate nomen Domini.

Sit nomen Domini benedictum, * ex hoc nunc et usque in sæculum.

A solis ortu usque ad occasum, * laudabile nomen Domini.

Excelsus super omnes gentes Dominus, * et super cœlos gloria ejus.

The Lord hath sworn, and he will not repent : Thou art a priest for ever according to the order of Melchisedech.

The Lord at thy right hand, hath broken kings in the day of his wrath.

He shall judge among nation, he shall fill ruins : he shall crush the heads in the land of many.

He shall drink of the torrent in the way : therefore shall he lift up the head.

Glory be to the Father, and to the Son, and to the Holy Ghost.

As it was in the beginning, is now, and ever shall be, world without end. Amen.

Ant. While the King was on his couch, my spikenard yielded a sweet odour.

Ant. His left hand under my head : and his right shall embrace me.

Psalm 112.

Praise the Lord, ye children : praise ye the name of the Lord.

Blessed be the name of the Lord : from henceforth now and for ever.

From the rising of the sun, until the going down of the same, the name of the Lord is worthy of praise.

The Lord is high above all nations : and his glory above the heavens.

Quis sicut Dominus Deus noster, qui in altis habitat, * et humilia respicit in cœlo et in terra ?

Suscitans a terra inopem, * et de stercore erigens pauperem :

Ut collocet eum cum principibus, * cum principibus populi sui.

Qui habitare facit sterilem in domo, *. matrem filiorum lætantem.

Gloria Patri, et Filio, * et Spiritui Sancto.

Sicut erat in principio, et nunc, et semper, * et in sæcula sæculorum. Amen.

Ant. Læva ejus sub capite meo, et dextera illius amplexabitur me.

Ant. Nigra sum, sed formosa, filiæ Jerusalem : ideo dilexit me Rex, et introduxit me in cubiculum suum.

Psalmus 121.

Lætatus sum in his, quæ dicta sunt mihi : * in domum Domini ibimus.

Stantes erant pedes nostri, * in atriis tuis Jerusalem.

Jerusalem quæ ædificatur ut civitas : * cujus participatio ejus in idipsum.

Illuc enim ascenderunt tribus, tribus

Who is as the Lord our God, who dwelleth on high : and looketh down on the low things in heaven and in earth ?

Raising up the needy from the earth, and lifting up the poor out of the dunghill:

That he may place him with princes, with the princes of his people.

Who maketh a barren woman to dwell in a house, the joyful mother of children.

Glory be to the Father, and to the Son, and to the Holy Ghost.

As it was in the beginning, is now, and ever shall be, world without end.   Amen.

Ant. His left hand under my head : and his right shall embrace me.

Ant. I am black but beautiful, O daughters of Jerusalem : therefore the King loved me and brought me into his chamber.

Psalm 121.

I rejoiced at the things that were said to me : We shall go into the house of the Lord.

Our feet were standing in thy courts, O Jerusalem.

Jerusalem, which is built as a city, which is compact together.

For thither did the tribes go up, the

Domini, * testimonium Israel, ad confitendum nomini Domini.

Quia illic sederunt sedes in judicio, * sedes super domum David.

Rogate quæ ad pacem sunt Jerusalem : * et abundantia diligentibus te.

Fiat pax in virtute tua : * et abundantia in turribus tuis.

Propter fratres meos, et proximos meos, * loquebar pacem de te.

Propter domum Domini Dei nostri, * quæsivi bona tibi.

Gloria Patri, et Filio, * et Spiritui Sancto.

Sicut erat in principio, et nunc, et semper, * et in sæcula sæculorum. Amen.

Ant. Nigra sum, sed formosa, filiæ Jerusalem : ideo dilexit me Rex, et introduxit me in cubiculum suum.

Ant. Jam hiems transiit, imber abiit, et recessit : surge, amica mea, et veni.

Psalmus 126.

Nisi Dominus ædificaverit domum, * in vanum laboraverunt qui ædificat eam.

Nisi Dominus custodierit civitatem, * frustra vigilat qui custodit eam.

tribes of the Lord : the testimony of Israel,
to praise the name of the Lord.

Because their seats have sat in judg-
ment, seats upon the house of David.

Pray ye for the things that are for the
peace of Jerusalem : and abundance for
them that love thee.

Let peace be in thy strength : and
abundance in thy towers.

For the sake of my brethren, and of my
neighbours, I spoke peace of thee.

Because of the house of the Lord our
God, I have sought good things for thee.

Glory be to the Father, and to the Son,
and to the Holy Ghost.

As it was in the beginning, is now, and
ever shall be, world without end. Amen.

Ant. I am black but beautiful, O daughters of Jerusalem : therefore the King
loved me and brought me into his
chamber.

Ant. Now the winter is past, the rain
over and gone: arise my beloved and come.

Psalm 126.

Unless the Lord build the house, they
labour in vain that build it.

Unless the Lord keep the city, he
watcheth in vain that keepeth it.

Vanum est vobis ante lucem surge : * surgite postquam sederitis, qui manducatis panem doloris.

Cum dederit dilectis suis somnum : * ecce hæreditas Domini, filii : merces, fructus ventris.

Sicut sagittæ in manu potentis : * ita filii excussorum.

Beatus vir qui implevit desiderium suum ex ipsis : * non confundetur cum loquetur inimicis suis in porta.

Gloria Patri, et Filio, * et Spiritui Sancto.

Sicut erat in principio, et nunc, et semper, * et in sæcula sæculorum. Amen.

Ant. Jam hiems transiit, imber abiit, et recessit : surge, amica mea, et veni.

Ant. Speciosa facta es, et suavis in deliciis tuis, sancta Dei genitrix.

Psalmus 147.

Lauda, Jerusalem, Dominum : * lauda Deum tuum, Sion.

Quoniam confortavit seras portarum tuarum : * benedixit filiis tuis in te.

It is vain for you to rise before light : rise ye after you have sitten, you that eat the bread of sorrow.

When he shall give sleep to his beloved : behold the inheritance of the Lord are children ; the reward, the fruit of the womb.

As arrows in the hand of the mighty, so the children of them that have been shaken.

Blessed is the man that hath filled his desire with them; he shall not be confounded when he shall speak to his enemies in the gate.

Glory be to the Father, and to the Son, and to the Holy Ghost.

As it was in the beginning, is now, and ever shall be, world without end. Amen.

Ant. Now the winter is past, the rain over and gone: arise my beloved and come.

Ant. Thou art beautiful and sweet in thy perfumes, O Sacred Mother of God.

Psalm 147.

Praise the Lord, O Jerusalem : praise thy God O Sion.

Because he hath strengthened the bolts of thy gates, he hath blessed thy children within thee.

Qui posuit fines tuos pacem : * et adipe frumenti satiat te.

Qui emittit eloquium suum terræ : * velociter currit sermo ejus.

Qui dat nivem, sicut lanam : * nebulam sicut cinerem spargit.

Mittit crystallum suam sicut buccellas : * ante faciem frigoris ejus quis sustinebit?

Emittet verbum suum, et liquefaciet ea : * flabit spiritus ejus, et fluent aquæ.

Qui annuntiat verbum suum Jacob, * justitias et judicia sua Israel.

Non fecit taliter omni nationi : * et judicia sua non manifestavit eis.

Gloria Patri, et Filio, * et Spiritui Sancto.

Sicut erat in principio, et nunc, et semper, * et in sæcula sæculorum. Amen.

Ant. Speciosa facta es, et suavis in deliciis tuis sancta Dei genitrix.

Capitulum—Eccli. 24.

Ab initio, et ante sæcula creata sum, et usque ad futurum sæculum non desinam, et in habitatione sancta coram ipso ministravi. R. Deo gratias.

Who hath placed peace in thy borders: and filled thee with the fat of corn.

Who sendeth forth his speech to the earth: his word runneth swiftly.

Who giveth snow like wool: scattereth mists like ashes.

He sendeth his crystal like morsels: who shall stand before the face of his cold?

He shall send out his word, and shall melt them: his wind shall blow, and the waters shall run.

Who declareth his word to Jacob: his justices and his judgments to Israel.

He hath not done in like manner to every nation: and his judgments he hath not made manifest to them.

Glory be to the Father, and to the Son, and to the Holy Ghost.

As it was in the beginning, is now, and ever shall be, world without end. Amen.

Ant. Thou art beautiful and sweet in thy perfumes, O Sacred Mother of God.

Little Chapter—Ecclus. 24.

From the beginning, and before the world was I created, and unto the world to come I shall not cease to be: in the holy dwelling place I ministered before him. R. Thanks be to God.

HYMNUS.

Ave, maris stella,
Dei Mater alma,
Atque semper virgo,
Felix cœli porta.

Sumens illud Ave
Gabrielis ore,
Funda nos in pace,
Mutans Hevæ nomen.

Solve vincla reis,
Profer lumen cæcis,
Mala nostra pelle,
Bona cuncta posce.

Monstra te esse matrem,
Sumat per te preces
Qui pro nobis natus,
Tulit esse tuus.

Virgo singularis,
Inter omnes mitis.
Nos culpis solutos
Mites fac et castos.

Vitam præsta puram,
Iter para tutum,
Ut videntes Jesum
Semper collætemur.

HYMN.

Gentle Star of ocean !
  Portal of the sky !
Ever Virgin Mother
  Of the Lord most High !

Oh ! by Gabriel's Ave,
  Utter'd long ago !
Eva's name reversing,
  'Stablish peace below.

Break the captive's fetters ;
  Light on blindness pour ;
All our ills expelling,
  Every bliss implore.

Show thyself a Mother ;
  Offer Him our sighs,
Who for us Incarnate
  Did not thee despise.

Virgin of all Virgins !
  To thy shelter take us ;
Gentlest of the gentle !
  Chaste and gentle make us.

Still as on we journey,
  Help our weak endeavour ;
Till with thee and Jesus
  We rejoice for ever.

Sit laus Deo Patri,
Summo Christo decus,
Spiritui sancto,
Tribus honor únus. *Amen.*

V. Dignare me laudare te, Virgo sacrata.

R. Da mihi virtutem contra hostes tuos.

Ad Magnif.

Ant. Sancta Maria, succurre miseris, juva pusillanimes, refove flebiles, ora pro populo, interveni pro clero, intercede pro devoto femineo sexu : sentiant omnes tuum juvamen quicumque celebrant tuam sanctam commemorationem.

Magnificat.

Magnificat * anima mea Dominum.

Et exultavit spiritus meus : * in Deo salutari meo.

Quia respexit humilitatem ancillæ suæ : * ecce enim ex hoc, beatam me dicent omnes generationes.

Quia fecit mihi magna qui potens est : * et sanctum nomen ejus.

Et misericordia ejus à progenie in progenies, * timentibus eum.

Fecit potentiam in brachio suo : * dispersit superbos mente cordis sui.

Through the highest heaven,
To the Almighty Three,
Father, Son, and Spirit
One same glory be. *Amen.*

V. Vouchsafe, O Sacred Virgin, to accept my praises.

R. Give me strength against thine enemies.

At the Magnificat.

Ant. Holy Mary, succour the miserable, help the dejected, comfort the afflicted, pray for the people, mediate for the clergy, intercede for the devout female sex, let all be sensible of thy help who celebrate thy holy commemoration.

Song of the B. V. Mary. Luke i. 46.

My soul doth magnify the Lord.

And my spirit hath rejoiced in God my Saviour.

Because he hath regarded the humility of his handmaid: for behold from henceforth all generations shall call me blessed.

Because he that is mighty hath done great things to me: and holy is his name.

And his mercy is from generation unto generation, to them that fear him.

He hath showed might in his arm: he

2

Deposuit potentes de sede : * et exalta-
vit humiles.

Esurientes implevit bonis : * et divites
dimisit inanes.

Suscepit Israel puerum suum : * recorda-
tus misericordiæ suæ.

Sicut· locutus est ad patres nostros : *
Abraham, et semini ejus in sæcula.

Gloria Patri, et Filio, * et Spiritui
Sancto.

Sicut erat in principio, et nunc, et
semper, * et in sæcula sæculorum. Amen.

Ant. Sancta Maria succurre miseris,
juva pusillanimes, refove flebiles, ora pro
populo, interveni pro clero, intercede pro
devoto femineo sexu : sentiant omnes
tuum juvamen, quicumque celebrant tuam
sanctam commemorationem.

V. Dominus vobiscum.

R. Et cum spiritu tuo.

Oremus.

Concede, quæsumus omnipotens Deus,
ut fideles tui, qui sub Sanctissimæ Virginis
Mariæ nomine et protectione lætantur, ejus
pia intercessione a cunctis malis liberentur
in terris, et ad gaudia æterna pervenire
mereantur in cœlis ; Per Dominum nostrum Jesum Christum Filium Tuum, Qui

hath scattered the proud in the conceit of their heart.

He hath put down the mighty ones from their seat: and hath exalted the humble.

He hath filled the hungry with good things: and the rich he hath sent empty away.

He hath received Israel, his servant: being mindful of his mercy.

As he spoke to our fathers: to Abraham and to his seed for ever.

Glory be to the Father, and to the Son, and to the Holy Ghost.

As it was in the beginning, is now, and ever shall be, world without end. Amen.

Ant. O Holy Mary, succour the miserable, help the dejected, comfort the afflicted, pray for the people, mediate for the clergy, intercede for the devout female sex, let all be sensible of thy help who celebrate thy holy commemoration.

V. The Lord be with you.

R. And with thy spirit.

Let us pray.

Grant, O Almighty God, that thy faithful who rejoice in the name and protection of the most holy Virgin Mary, may, by her pious intercession, be delivered

tecum vivit et regnat in unitate Spiritus
Sancti Deus, per omnia sæcula sæculorum.
Amen.

V. Dominus vobiscum.

R. Et cum spiritu tuo.

V. Benedicamus Domino.

R. Deo gratias.

V. Fidelium animæ per misericordiam
Dei requiescant in pace.

R. Amem.

Pater Noster *(Secreto)*.

V. Dominus det nobis suam pacem.

R. Et vitam æternam.   Amen.

ANTIPHONÆ PRO TEMPORE.

*A Vesperis Sabbati ante Dominicam primam Adven-
tus, usque ad Purificationem inclusive.*

Antiphona.

Alma Redemptoris mater, quæ pervia cœli
Porta manes, et stella maris, succurre
    cadenti
Surgere qui curat, populo: tu quæ genuisti,
Natura mirante, tuum sanctum Genitorem,
Virgo prius ac posterius, Gabrielis ab ore
Sumens illud Ave peccatorum miserere.

In Adventu.

V. Angelus Domini nuntiavit Mariæ.

R. Et concepit de Spiritu sancto.

from all earthly evils, and deserve to obtain
the eternal joys of heaven, through our
Lord Jesus Christ. Amen.

V. The Lord be with you.

R. And with thy spirit.

V. Let us bless the Lord.

R. Thanks be to God.

V. May the souls of the faithful, through
the mercy of God, rest in peace.

R. Amen.

Our Father *(in Secret)*.

V. The Lord give us his peace.

R. And eternal life. Amen.

ANTHEMS FOR PARTICULAR PERIODS OF THE YEAR.

*Anthem from the First Sunday of Advent till the
Purification.*

Mother of Jesus, heaven's open gate,
Star of the sea, support the falling state
Of mortals; thou, whose womb thy
    Maker bore,   [fore.
And yet (strange thing!) a Virgin as be-
Who didst from Gabriel's "Hail!" the
    news receive,
Repenting sinners by thy prayers relieve.

V. The angel of the Lord declared unto
Mary,

R. And she conceived by the Holy Ghost.

Oremus.

Gratiam tuam, quæsumus Domine, mentibus nostris infunde : ut qui, Angelo nuntiante, Christi Filii tui incarnationem cognovimus, per passionem ejus et crucem ad resurrectionis gloriam perducamur, per eumdem Christum Dominum nostrum.

R. Amen.

A primis Vesperis Nativitatis et deinceps.

V. Post partum virgo inviolata permansisti.

R. Dei Genitrix, intercede pro nobis.

Oremus.

Deus, qui salutis æternæ, beatæ Mariæ virginitate fœcunda, humano generi præmia præstitisti : tribue quæsumus ; ut ipsam pro nobis intercedere sentiamus, per quam meruimus auctorem vitæ suscipere Dominum nostrum Jesum Christum Filium tuum. *R.* Amen.

Post Purificationem, i.e. a fine Completorii illius diei inclusive, usque ad Feriam quintam in Cœna Domini exclusive.

Antiphona.

Ave Regina Cœlorum,
Ave Domina Angelorum.
Salve radix, salve porta
Ex qua mundo lux est orta :

Let us Pray.

Pour forth, we beseech thee, O Lord, thy grace into our hearts; that we, to whom the incarnation of Christ thy Son was made known by the message of an angel, may, by his passion and cross, be brought to the glory of his resurrection, through the same Christ our Lord. Amen.

From the first Vespers of Christmas-day is said,

V. After child-birth, thou didst remain a pure virgin.

R. O Mother of God, intercede for us.

Let us Pray.

O God, who by the fruitful virginity of blessed Mary, hast given to mankind the rewards of eternal salvation: grant, we beseech thee, that we may experience her intercession, by whom we received the Author of life, our Lord Jesus Christ thy Son. Amen.

Anthem from the Purification till Maundy Thursday.

Hail, Mary, Queen of heavenly spheres!
Hail, whom the angelic host reveres!
Hail, fruitful root! Hail, sacred gate,
Whence the world's light derives its date!

Gaude virgo gloriosa,
Super omnes speciosa :
Vale ô valdè decora,
Et pro nobis Christum exora.

V. Dignare me laudare te, Virgo sacrata.
R. Da mihi virtutem contra hostes tuos.

Oremus.

Concede, misericors Deus, fragilitati nostræ præsidium : ut qui sanctæ Dei Genitricis memoriam agimus, intercessionis ejus auxilio a nostris iniquitatibus resurgamus, per eumdem Christum Dominum nostrum. *R.* Amen.

A Completorio Sabbati sancti usque ad Nonam Sabbati post Pentecosten inclusive.

Antiphona.

Regina cœli lætare, alleluia.
Quia quem meruisti portare, alleluia.
Resurrexit sicut dixit, alleluia.
Ora pro nobis Deum, alleluia.

V. Gaude et lætare virgo Maria, alleluia.
R. Quia surrexit Dominus vere, alleluia.

Oremus.

Deus, qui per resurrectionem Filii tui Domini nostri Jesu Christi mundum lætificare dignatus es : præsta quæsumus ; ut per ejus genitricem Virginem Mariam perpetuæ capiamus gaudia vitæ, per

O glorious maid, with beauty blest!
May joys eternal fill thy breast!
Thus crowned with beauty and with joy,
Thy prayers for us with Christ employ.

V. Vouchsafe, O sacred Virgin, to accept my praises.

R. Give me strength against thine enemies.

Let us pray.

Grant us, O merciful God, strength against our enemies; that we who celebrate the memory of the holy Mother of God, may be enabled to rise again from our iniquities. Through the same Christ our Lord. Amen.

Anthem from Holy Saturday till Trinity-Eve.

Triumph, O Queen of heaven, to see
The sacred Infant born of thee,
Return in glory from the tomb,
And with thy prayers prevent our doom.

V. Rejoice, and be glad, O Virgin Mary. Alleluia.

R. For the Lord is truly risen. Alleluia.

Let us Pray.

O God, who hast deigned, by the resurrection of thy Son our Lord Jesus Christ, to fill the world with joy; grant,

eumdem Christum Dominum nostrum.
R. Amen.

A primis Vesperis Festi Trinitatis usque ad Nonam Sabbati ante Adventum.

Antiphona.

Salve Regina, mater misericordiæ ;
Vita, dulcedo, et spes nostra, salve.
Ad te clamamus exules, filii Hevæ.
Ad te suspiramus gementes et flentes in hac
lacrymarum valle.
Eia ergo, advocata nostra,
Illos tuos misericordes oculos ad nos converte.
Et Jesum benedictum fructum ventris tui,
Nobis post hoc exilium ostende,
O clemens, ô pia, ô dulcis virgo Maria.

V. Ora pro nobis sancta Dei genitrix.
R. Ut digni efficiamur promissionibus
Christi.

Oremus.

Omnipotens sempiterne Deus, qui glori-
osæ virginis matris Mariæ corpus et ani-
mam, ut dignum Filii tui habitaculum
effici mereretur, Spiritu sancto cooperante
præparasti : da ut cujus commemoratione
lætamur, ejus pia intercessione ab instanti-
bus malis, et a morte perpetua liberemur,
per eumdem Christum Dominum nostrum.
R. Amen.

V. Divinum auxilium maneat semper
nobiscum. *R.* Amen.

we beseech thee, that through His Virgin
Mother, Mary, we may receive the joys of
eternal life. Through, &e. Amen.

Anthem from Trinity-Eve till Advent.

Hail happy Queen, thou mercy's parent hail.
Life, hope, and comfort of this earthly vale.
To thee we, Eva's wretched children cry
In sighs and tears, to thee we suppliants fly.
Rise, glorious advocate, exert thy love,
And let our vows those eyes of pity move.
O sweet, O pious maid ! for us obtain,
For us who long have in our exile lain,
To see thy infant Jesus, and with Him to reign.

V. Pray for us, O holy Mother of God.

R. That we may be made worthy of the
promises of Christ.

Let us pray.

Almighty and eternal God, who by the
co-operation of the Holy Ghost, didst pre-
pare the body and soul of the Glorious
Virgin Mother Mary, that she might
become a worthy habitation for thy Son ;
grant that, as with joy we celebrate her
memory, so by her pious intercesion we
may be delivered from present evils, and
eternal death. Through, &c. Amen.

V. May the divine assistance remain
always with us. *R.* Amen.

HYMNS.

Paradise.

1 O Paradise! O Paradise!
    Who doth not crave for rest?
Who would not seek the happy land,
    Where they that loved are blest;

      Where loyal hearts and true,
        Stand ever in the light
      All rapture through and through,
        In God's most holy sight?

2 O Paradise! O Paradise!
    Wherefore doth death delay ;
Bright death, that is the welcome dawn
    Of our eternal day;
      Where loyal hearts, and true, &c.

3 O Paradise! O Paradise!
    'Tis weary waiting here;
I long to be where Jesus is,
    To feel, to see Him near.
      Where loyal hearts, and true, &c.

4 O Paradise ! O Paradise!
    I want to sin no more !
I want to be as pure on earth
    As on thy spotless shore.
      Where loyal hearts, and true, &c.

5 O Paradise! O Paradise !
    I feel 'twill not be long ;
Patience ! I almost think I hear
    Faint fragments of thy song.
        Where loyal hearts, and true, &c.

Hymn of St. Bernard.

1 Jesus, the only thought of Thee,
    With sweetness fills my breast ;
But sweeter far it is to see,
    And on Thy beauty feast.

2 No sound, no harmony so gay,
    Can art or music frame ;
No thoughts can reach, no words can say,
    The sweets of Thy blest name.

3 Jesus, our hope, when we repent,
    Sweet source of all our grace :
Sole comfort in our banishment,
    Oh ! what when face to face!

4 Jesus, that name inspires my mind
    With springs of life and light;
More than I ask in Thee I find,
    And languish with delight.

5 No art or eloquence of man
    Can tell the joys of love;
Only the saints can understand
    What they in Jesus prove.

6 Thee, then, I'll seek, retired apart,
　　From world and business free ;
　When these shall knock, I'll shut my heart,
　　And keep it all for Thee.

7 Before the morning light I'll come,
　　With Magdalen, to find,
　In sighs and tears, my Jesu's tomb,
　　And there refresh my mind.

8 My tears upon His grave shall flow,
　　My sighs the garden fill ;
　Then at His feet myself I'll throw,
　　And there I'll seek His will.

9 Jesus, in Thy blest steps I'll tread,
　　And walk in all Thy ways;
　I'll never cease to weep and plead
　　Till I'm restored to grace.

10 O King of love, Thy blessed fire
　　Does such sweet flames excite,
　That first it raises the desire,
　　Then fills it with delight.

11 Thy lovely presence shines so clear
　　Through every sense and way,
　That souls which once have seen Thee near
　　See all things else decay.

12 Come, then, dear Lord, possess my heart,
　　Chase thence the shades of night;
　Come, pierce it with Thy flaming dart,
　　And ever shining light.

13 Sweet Jesus, Saviour, Lord and King,
　To Thee, through endless days,
My grateful heart and tongue shall sing
　Eternal hymns of praise.

The Sacred Heart.

1 To Jesus' Heart, all burning
　With fervent love for men,
My heart, with fondest yearning,
　Shall raise its joyful strain:

　　While ages course along,
　　Blest be, with loudest song,
　　The Sacred Heart of Jesus,
　　By every heart and tongue.

2 O Heart for me on fire
　With love no tongue can speak,
My yet untold desire
　God gives me for Thy sake.
　　While ages course along, &c.

3 Too true, I have forsaken
　Thy love by wilful sin ;
Yet now let me be taken
　Back by Thy grace again.
　　While ages course along, &c.

4 As Thou art meek and lowly,
　And ever pure of heart,
So may my heart be wholly
　Of Thine the counterpart.
　　While ages course along, &c.

5 Oh ! that to me were given
    The pinions of a dove,
I'd speed aloft to Heaven,
    My Jesus' love to prove.
        While ages course along, &c.

6 When life away is flying,
    And earth's false glare is done;
Still, Sacred Heart, in dying,
    I'll say I'm all Thine own.
        While ages course along, &c.

Sweet Sacrament.

1 Jesus, my Lord, my God, my all,
    How can I love Thee as I ought?
And how revere this wondrous gift,
    So far surpassing hope or thought ?
        Sweet Sacrament, we Thee adore;
        O make us love Thee more and more.

2 Had I but Mary's sinless heart
    To love Thee with, my dearest King;
Oh ! with what bursts of fervent praise
    Thy goodness, Jesus, would I sing !
        Sweet Sacrament, &c.

3 Oh ! see, within a creature's hand
    The vast Creator deigns to be,
Reposing infant-like, as though
    On Joseph's arm, or Mary's knee.
        Sweet Sacrament, &c.

4 Thy Body, Soul, and Godhead all,—
  O mystery of love divine!
I cannot compass all I have,
  For all Thou hast and art are mine.
            Sweet Sacrament, &c.

5 Sound, sound His praises higher still,
  And come, ye angels, to our aid,
'Tis God! 'tis God! the very God
  Whose power both man and angels made!
  Sweet Sacrament! we Thee adore!
  O make us love Thee more and more.

Veni, Creator Spiritus.

1 Come, Holy Ghost, Creator, come,
  From Thy bright heavenly throne;
Come, take possession of our souls,
  And make them all Thy own.

2 Thou who art called the Paraclete,
  Best gift of God above;
The living Spring, the living Fire,
  Sweet Unction and true Love.

3 Thou who art sevenfold in Thy grace,
  Finger of God's right hand;
His promise teaching little ones
  To speak and understand.

4 Oh! guide our minds with Thy blest light,
  With love our hearts inflame;
3

And with Thy strength, which ne'er decays,
  Confirm our mortal frame.

5 Far from us drive our hellish foe,
    True peace unto us bring;
  And through all perils lead us safe
    Beneath Thy sacred wing.

6 Through Thee may we the Father know,
    Through Thee th' Eternal Son,
  And Thee the Spirit of Them both,
    Thrice blessed Three in One.

7 All glory to the Father be,
    With His coequal Son;
  The like to Thee, great Paraclete,
    Till time itself is done.   Amen.

Veni, Sancte Spiritus.

1 Come, Holy Ghost, send down those beams
  Which sweetly flow in silent streams
    From Thy bright throne above;
  O come, Thou Father of the poor;
  O come, Thou source of all our store;
    Come, fill our hearts with love.

2 O Thou of comforters the best;
  O Thou, the soul's delightful guest,
    The pilgrim's sweet relief;
  Thou art true rest in toil and sweat,
  Refreshment in excess of heat,
    And solace in our grief.

3 Thrice-blessed light, shoot home Thy darts,
  And pierce the centres of those hearts
    Whose faith aspires to Thee ;
  Without Thy Godhead nothing can
  Have any price or worth in man,
    Nothing can harmless be.

4 Lord, wash our sinful stains away,
  Refresh from heaven our barren clay,
    Our wounds and bruises heal ;
  To Thy sweet yoke our stiff necks bow,
  Warm with Thy fire our hearts of snow,
    Our wand'ring feet repeal.

5 Grant to Thy faithful, dearest Lord,
  Whose only hope is Thy sure word,
    The seven gifts of Thy Spirit;
  Grant us in life Thy helping grace,
  Grant us at death to see Thy face,
    And endless joy inherit.

Act of Contrition.

1 God of mercy and compassion,
    Look with pity down on me;
  Father, let me call Thee Father,
    'Tis Thy child returns to Thee.

      Jesus, Lord, I ask for mercy,
        Let me not implore in vain;
      All my sins, I now detest them,
        Never will I sin again.

2 By my sins I have deservèd
   Death and endless misery,
Hell with all its pains and torments,
   And for all eternity.
               Jesus, Lord, &c.

3 By my sins I have abandoned
   Right and claim to heaven above,
Where the Saints rejoice for ever
   In a boundless sea of love.
               Jesus, Lord, &c.

4 See our Saviour, bleeding, dying,
   On the cross of Calvary;
To that cross my sins have nailed Him,
   Yet He bleeds and dies for me.
               Jesus, Lord, &c.

O, Flower of Grace.

1 O Flower of Grace, divinest Flower,
God's light thy life, God's love thy dower;
That all alone, with virgin ray,
Dost make in heaven eternal May ;
Sweet falls the peerless dignity,
Of God's eternal choice on thee.

   Mother dearest, Mother fairest;
   Maiden purest, Maiden rarest;
   Help of earth and joy of heaven;
   Love and praise to thee be given,
     Blissful Mother, blissful Maiden.

2 Choice flower, that bloomest on the breast
Of Jesus, which is now thy rest,
As thine was once the chosen bed
Of His dear Heart and sacred Head;
O Mary, sweet it is to see
Thy Son's creation graced by thee.
Mother dearest, &c.

3 O Flower of God, divinest Flower,
Elected for His inmost bower ;
Where angels come not, there art thou,
A crown of glory on thy brow;
While far below, all bright and brave,
Their gleamy palms the ransomed wave.
Mother dearest, &c.

4 O Mary, when we think of thee,
Our hearts grow light as light can be;
For thou hast felt as we have felt,
And thou hast knelt as we have knelt;
And so it is that, utterly,
Mother of God, we trust in thee.
Mother dearest, &c.

Ave Maris Stella.

1 Hail, Queen of Heaven, the ocean Star,
Guide of the wanderer here below,
Thrown on life's surge, we claim thy care;
Save us from peril and from woe.
Mother of Christ, Star of the sea,
Pray for the wanderer, pray for me.

2　O gentle, chaste, and spotless Maid,
　　We sinners make our prayers through thee;
　Remind thy Son that He has paid
　　　The price of our iniquity.
　　　　Virgin most pure, Star of the sea,
　　　　Pray for the sinner, pray for me.

3　Sojourners in this vale of tears,
　　To thee, blest Advocate, we cry;
　Pity our sorrows, calm our fears,
　　　And soothe with hope our misery.
　　　　Refuge in grief, Star of the sea,
　　　　Pray for the mourner, pray for me.

4　And while to HIM who reigns above,
　　In Godhead One, in Persons Three,
　The source of life, of grace, of love,
　　　Homage we pay on bended knee,
　　　　Do thou, bright Queen, Star of the sea,
　　　　Pray for thy children, pray for me.

St. Casimir's Hymn.

1　Daily, daily sing to Mary,
　　Sing, my soul, her praises due,
　All her feasts, her actions worship
　　With the heart's devotion true.
　Lost in wond'ring contemplation,
　　Be her Majesty confest:
　Call her Mother, call her Virgin,
　　Happy Mother, Virgin blest.

2 She is mighty to deliver;
  Call her, trust her lovingly:
When the tempest rages round thee,
  She will calm the troubled sea.
Gifts of Heaven she has given,
  Noble lady! to our race:
She, the Queen, who decks her subjects
  With the light of God's own grace.

3 Sing, my tongue, the Virgin's trophies,
  Who for us her Maker bore;
For the curse of old inflicted,
  Peace and blessing to restore.
Sing in songs of praise unending,
  Sing the world's majestic Queen;
Weary not, nor faint in telling
  All the gifts she gives to men.

4 All my senses, heart, affections,
  Strive to sound her glory forth:
Spread abroad the sweet memorials
  Of the Virgin's priceless worth.
Where the voice of music thrilling?
  Where the tongue of eloquence,
That can utter hymns beseeming
  All her matchless excellence?

5 All our joys do flow from Mary,
  All then join her praise to sing:
Trembling sing the Virgin Mother,
  Mother of our Lord and King.

While we sing her awful glory,
　Far above our fancy's reach,
Let our hearts be quick to offer
　Love the heart alone can teach.

The Month of May.

1 Dear Mother! make me love to pray
　To thee in thy sweet Month of May,
　And kneel before thee every day,
　　Our holy Queen!

2 Thine altars shall be ever green,
　May's sweetest flowers shall there be seen,
　And tapers' light shall hail the Queen
　　Of the Month of May.

3 My mother she may cease to love,
　My earthly friends unfaithful prove,
　But not my Mother up above,
　　Our holy Queen.

5 What heaven is I cannot say,
　But, oh! it must be like to May,
　For there they honour every day
　　Our holy Queen.

The Month of November.

1 Oh! turn to Jesus, Mother! turn,
　　And call Him by His tenderest names;
Pray for the Holy Souls that burn
　　This hour amid the cleansing flames.

Ah! they have fought a gallant fight,
  In death's cold arms they persevered;
And after life's uncheery night
  The harbour of their rest is neared.

2 They are the children of thy tears;
  Then hasten, Mother! to their aid;
In pity think each hour appears
  An age while glory is delayed.
Ah me! the love of Jesus yearns
  O'er that abyss of sacred pain,
And as He looks His Bosom burns
  With Calvary's dear thirst again.

3 O Mary! let thy Son no more
  · His lingering Spouses thus expect;
God's children to their God restore,
  And to the Spirit His elect.
Pray, then, as thou hast ever prayed;
  Angels and Souls, all look to thee;
God waits thy prayers, for He hath made
  Those prayers His law of charity.

St. Dominic.

Patron of the Confraternity of the Holy Rosary.

1 Thou who hero-like hast striven,
  For the cause of God and heaven,
Dominic, whose life was given
    Sinners to recall.

2 Saint of high and dauntless spirit,
By thy vast unmeasured merit,
By thy name which we inherit,
    Hear us when we call.

3 Flower of chastity the fairest
Of her lily buds thou bearest,
Snow white as the robe thou wearest
    Gift from hands divine.

4 With thy brow of starry splendour,
With thine eyes so mild and tender,
Mary's client—truth's defender,
    To our prayers incline.

5 Great Apostle ever claiming
Souls for Jesus—by the naming,
Mary and her Son proclaiming
    Mysteries of faith.

6 Still, O Dominic, the preaching
Of those child-like beads is reaching
Child-like hearts, all sweetly teaching,
    Christ's own life and death.

7 With those Aves, first and plainest
Of the Church's prayers, thou rainest
Blessings on the earth, and gainest
    Souls whom Jesus made.

8 Loving Father! at thy station
Of seraphic contemplation
In each hour of dark temptation,
    Give thy saving aid.

Faith of our Fathers.

1 Faith of our Fathers! living still,
  In spite of dungeon, fire, and sword;
O, how our hearts beat high with joy
  Whene'er we hear that glorious word!
Faith of our Fathers! holy Faith,
We will be true to thee till death.

2 Our fathers, chained in prisons dark,
  Were still in heart and conscience free;
How sweet would be their children's fate,
  If they, like them, could die for thee!
Faith of our Fathers! holy Faith,
We will be true to thee till death.

3 Faith of our Fathers! Mary's prayers
  Shall win this country back to thee;
And through the truth that comes from God,
  This land shall then indeed be free.
Faith of our Fathers! holy Faith,
We will be true to thee till death.

4 Faith of our Fathers! we will love
  Both friend and foe in all our strife;
And preach thee, too, as love knows how,
  By kindly words and virtuous life.
Faith of our Fathers! holy Faith,
We will be true to thee till death.

For the Stations of the Cross.

Sancta Mater, istud agas,
Crucifixi fige plagas
Cordi meo valide.

My Jesus! who, for love of me,
Didst bear Thy cross to Calvary,
In Thy sweet mercy grant to me
To suffer and to die for Thee.

Heaven is the Prize.

1 Yes, heaven is the prize,
My soul shall strive to gain,
One glimpse of Paradise
Repays a life of pain :

'Tis heaven !—'tis heaven!—yes,
Heaven is the prize !

2 Yes, heaven is the prize !
My soul, oh think of this !
All earthly goods despise,
For such a crown of bliss.
'Tis heaven, &c.

3 Yes, heaven is the prize!
When sorrows press around,
Look up beyond the skies
Where hope and strength are found.
'Tis heaven, &c.

4 Yes, heaven is the prize !
 Oh, 'tis not hard to gain,
He surely wins who tries:—
 For hope can conquer pain.
   'Tis heaven, &c.

5 Yes, heaven is the prize!
 The strife will soon be past,
Faint not! but raise your eyes
 And struggle to the last.
   'Tis heaven, &c.

6 Yes, heaven is the prize!
 Faith shows the crown to gain,—
Hope lights the way and dies—
 But love will always reign.
   'Tis heaven, &c.

7 Yes, heaven is the prize!
 Too much cannot be given,
And he alone is wise
 Who gives up *all* for heaven.
   'Tis heaven, &o.

8 Yes, heaven is the prize!
 Death opens wide the door,
And then the spirit flies
 To God for evermore.
'Tis heaven!—'tis heaven!—yes,
 Heaven is the prize!

Evening Hymn.

1 Sweet Saviour! bless us ere we go;
    Thy word into our minds instil:
And make our lukewarm hearts to glow
    With lowly love and fervent will.
Through life's long day and death's dark
    night
O gentle Jesus! be our light!

2 The day is done, its hours have run;
    And Thou hast taken count of all—
The scanty triumphs grace hath won,
    The broken vow, the frequent fall.
Through life's long day and death's dark
O gentle Jesus! be our light!   [night

3 Grant us, dear Lord! from evil ways
    True absolution and release;
And bless us more than in past days
    With purity and inward peace.
Through life's long day and death's dark
O gentle Jesus! be our light.   [night

4 Do more than pardon; give us joy,
    Sweet fear and sober liberty;
And simple hearts without alloy,
    That only long to be like Thee.
Through life's long day and death's dark
    night
O gentle Jesus! be our light!

5 Labour is sweet, for Thou hast toiled;
    And care is light, for Thou hast cared:
Ah! never let our works be soiled
    With strife, or by deceit ensnared.
Through life's long day and death's dark
O gentle Jesus! be our light.   [night

6 For all we love, the poor, the sad,
    The sinful—unto Thee we call;
O let Thy mercy make us glad:
    Thou art our Jesus and our All.
Through life's long day and death's dark
    night
O gentle Jesus! be our light!

7 Sweet Saviour! bless us; night is come,
    Mary and Joseph near us be ;
Good angels, watch about our home;
    May we each day be nearer Thee!
Through life's long day and death's dark
    night
O gentle Jesus! be our light!

God bless our Pope.

1 Full in the panting heart of Rome,
Beneath the Apostle's crowning dome,
From pilgrims' lips that kiss the ground,
Breathes in all tongues one only sound :
" God bless our Pope, the great, the good."

2 The golden roof, the marble walls,
  The Vatican's majestic halls,   .
  The note redouble ; till it fills
  With echoes sweet the seven hills;
  " God bless our Pope, the great, the good."

3 Then surging through each hallowed gate,
  Where martyrs glory, in peace, await,
  It sweeps beyond the solemn plain,
  Peals over Alps, across the main:
  " God bless our Pope, the great, the good."

4 From torrid South to frozen North,
  The wave harmonious stretches forth;   .
  Yet strikes no chord more true to Rome's,
  Than rings within our hearts and homes:
  " God bless our Pope, the great, the good."

5 For like the sparks of unseen fire,
  That speak along the magic wire,
  From home to home, from heart to heart,
  These words of countless children dart:
  " God bless our Pope, the great, the good."

Evening Hymn.

1 Hear Thy children, gentle Jesus,
    While we breathe our evening prayer,
  Save us from all harm and danger,
    Take us 'neath Thy shelt'ring care.

2 Save us from the wiles of Satan,
    'Mid the lone and sleepful night,

Sweetly may bright guardian angels
    Keep us 'neath their watchful sight.

3 Gentle Jesus, look in pity
    From Thy glorious throne above,
All the night Thy heart is wakeful
    In Thy Sacrament of love.

4 Shades of even fast are falling,
    Day is fading into gloom,
When the shades of death fall round us,
    Lead Thine exiled children home

Mother of Mercy.

1 Mother of Mercy, day by day
    My love of thee grows more and more;
Thy gifts are strewn upon my way,
    Like sands upon the great sea shore.

2 Though poverty and work and woe
    The masters of my life may be,
When times are worst, who does not know
    Darkness is light with love of thee!

3 But scornful men have coldly said
    Thy love was leading me from God,
And yet in this I did but tread
    The very path my Saviour trod.

4 They know but little of thy worth
    Who speak these heartless words to me;
For what did Jesus love on earth
    One half so tenderly as thee?
4.

5 Get me the grace to love thee more;
 Jesus will give if thou wilt plead;
And, Mother, when life's cares are o'er,
 Oh, I shall love thee then indeed.

6 Jesus, when His three hours were run,
 Bequeathed thee from the cross to me;
How can I rightly love thy Son,
 Sweet Mother! if I love not thee?

Hail! Thou Living Bread.

1 Hail, Thou living Bread from Heaven,
 Sacrament of awful might!
I adore Thee,—I adore Thee,—
 Every moment, day and night.

2 Holiest Jesus!—Heart of Jesus!
 O'er me shed your gifts divine:
Holiest Jesus! my Redeemer!
 All my heart and soul are Thine.

Maiden Mother.

1 Maiden Mother, meek and mild,
Take, oh take me for thy child.
All my life, oh let it be
My best joy to think of thee.

2· When my eyes are closed in sleep
Through the night my slumbers keep,
Make my latest thought to be
How to love thy Son and thee.

3 Teach me when the sunbeam bright
Calls me with its golden light,
How my waking thoughts may be
Turn'd to Jesus and to thee.

4 And, oh, teach me through the day
Oft to raise my heart and say,
" Maiden Mother, meek and mild,
Guide, oh, guide thy faithful child!"

5 Thus, sweet Mother, day and night
Thou shalt guide my steps aright ;
And my dying words shall be,
" Virgin Mother, pray for me !

Life Eternal.

1 Life eternal ! Life eternal !
Words that pierce the heart with fire !
Life eternal ! Life eternal !
How my soul doth thee desire !

2 Life eternal! Life eternal !
Hope of hopes to mortal man:
Life eternal ! Life eternal !
I will grasp thee if I can.

3 Life eternal ! Life eternal !
Depth of depth of bliss unknown !
Life eternal ! Life eternal !
Thee I seek in Christ alone.

Te Lucis.

1 Now with the fast-departing light,
    Maker of all ! we ask of Thee,
Of Thy great mercy, through the night
    Our guardian and defence to be.

2 Far off let idle visions fly;
    No phantom of the night molest;
Curb Thou our raging enemy,
    That we in chaste repose may rest.

3 Father of mercies, hear our cry ;
    Hear us, O sole-begotten Son :
Who with the Holy Ghost most high,
    Reignest while endless ages run.

The Loving Heart of Jesus.

1 The loving Heart of Jesus seek
    In trouble and distress,
Whatever sorrow vex the mind,
    Or guilt the soul oppress.

2 Jesus, who gave Himself for you
    Upon the Cross to die,
Opens to you His Sacred Heart—
    Oh, to that Heart draw nigh.

3 Ye hear how kindly He invites;
    Ye hear His words so blest—
" All ye that labour, come to Me,
    And I will give you rest."

4 What meeker than the Saviour's Heart?—
    As on the Cross He lay,
It did His murderers forgive,
    And for their pardon pray.

5 O Heart! thou joy of Saints on high!
    Thou hope of sinners here!
Attracted by those loving words,
    To Thee I lift my prayer.

6 Wash Thou my wounds in that dear Blood
    Which forth from Thee did flow;
New grace, new hope inspire ; a new
    And better heart bestow.

My God, how wonderful Thou art!

1 My God, how wonderful Thou art !
    Thy Majesty how bright!
How beautiful Thy mercy-seat
    In depths of burning light !
How dread are Thine eternal years,
    O everlasting Lord!
By prostrate spirits day and night
    Incessantly adored.

2 How wonderful, how beautiful
    The sight of Thee must be,
Thine endless wisdom, boundless power,
    And awful purity !

O, how I fear Thee, living God,
   With deepest, tend'rest fears,
And worship Thee with trembling hope
   And penitential tears.

3 Yet I may love Thee too, O Lord,
   Almighty as Thou art ;
For Thou hast stooped to ask of me
   The love of my poor heart.
No earthly father loves like Thee;
   No mother half so mild
Bears and forbears as Thou hast done
   With me Thy sinful child.

4 Only to sit and think of God,
   O what a joy it is !
To think the thoughts, to breathe the Name,
   Earth has no higher bliss.
Father of Jesus, love's Reward,
   What rapture will it be,
Prostrate before Thy throne to lie,
   And gaze and gaze on Thee !

𝔓rayer to 𝔍esus in the 𝔅lessed 𝔖acrament.

1 O Jesus Christ remember,
   When Thou shalt come again,
Upon the clouds of heaven,
   With all Thy shining train ;

2 When every eye shall see Thee
   In Deity reveal'd,

Who now upon this altar
In silence art concealed:—

3 Remember then, O Saviour,
   I supplicate of Thee,
That here I bow'd before Thee,
   Upon my bended knee;

4 That here I own'd Thy presence,
   And did not Thee deny;
And glorified Thy greatness,
   Though hid from human eye :

5 Accept, divine Redeemer,
   The homage of my praise;
Be Thou the light and honour,
   And glory of my days.

6 Be Thou my consolation
   When death is drawing nigh;
Be Thou my only treasure
   Through all eternity.

BENEDICTION OF
THE BLESSED SACRAMENT.

During this solemn Rite, all present kneel and adore our Divine Lord, really, truly, and substantially present in the Sacrament of the Altar.

Hymnus.

O Salutaris Hostia,
Quæ cœli pandis os-
   tium :
Bella premunt hosti-
   lia :
Da robur, fer auxili-
   um.

Uni trinoque Do-
   mino,
Sit sempiterna glo-
   ria :
Qui vitam sine ter-
   mino,
Nobis donet in pa-
   tria. Amen.

Hymn.

O Saving Host! that
   heaven's gate,
Laid'st open at so
   dear a rate :
Intestine wars in-
   vade our breast ;
Be thou our strength,
   support, and rest.

To God the Father,
   and the Son,
And Holy Spirit,
   Three in one,
Be endless praise :
   may HE above
With life eternal
   crown our love.
   Amen.

The Litany of the Blessed Virgin.

(Occasionally some other prayer, or hymn suitable to the particular festival, is substituted for this Litany.) `

Kyrie eleison.	Lord, have mercy on us.
Kyrie eleison.	*Lord, have mercy on us.*
Christe eleison.	Christ, have mercy on us.
Christe eleison.	*Christ, have mercy on us.*
Kyrie eleison.	Lord, have mercy on us.
Kyrie eleison.	*Lord, have mercy on us.*
Christe audi nos.	Christ, hear us.
Christe exaudi nos.	*Christ, graciously hear us.*
Pater de cœlis Deus, *miserere nobis.*	God, the Father of heaven, *Have mercy on us.*
Fili Redemptor mundi Deus, *miserere nobis.*	God, the Son, Redeemer of the world, *Have mercy on us.*
Spiritus Sancte Deus, *miserere nobis.*	God the Holy Ghost, *Have mercy on us.*

Sancta Trinitas, unus Deus, *miserere nobis.* — Holy Trinity, one God, *Have mercy on us.*

Sancta Maria, *ora pro nobis.* — Holy Mary, *Pray for us.*

Sancta Dei genitrix, — Holy Mother of God,

Sancta Virgo Virginum, — Holy Virgin of virgins,

Mater Christi, — Mother of Christ,

Mater divinæ gratiæ, — Mother of divine grace,

Mater purissima, — Mother most pure,

Mater castissima, — Mother most chaste,

Mater inviolata, — Mother inviolate,

Mater intemerata, — Mother undefiled,

Mater amabilis, — Mother most amiable,

Mater admirabilis, — Mother most admirable,

Mater Creatoris, — Mother of our Creator,

Mater Salvatoris, — Mother of our Redeemer,

Virgo prudentissima, — Virgin most prudent,

Virgo veneranda, — Virgin most venerable,

Ora pro nobis.

Pray for us.

Virgo prædicanda,	Virgin most renowned,
Virgo potens,	Virgin most powerful,
Virgo clemens,	Virgin most merciful,
Virgo fidelis,	Virgin most faithful,
Speculum Justitiæ,	Mirror of Justice,
Sedes sapientiæ,	Seat of wisdom,
Causa nostræ lætitiæ,	Cause of our joy,
Vas spirituale,	Spiritual Vessel,
Vas honorabile,	Vessel of honour,
Vas insigne devotionis,	Vessel of singular devotion,
Rosa mystica,	Mystical rose,
Turris Davidica,	Tower of David,
Turris eburnea,	Tower of ivory,
Domus aurea,	House of gold,
Fœderis arca,	Ark of the covenant,
Janua Cœli,	Gate of heaven,
Stella matutina,	Morning star,
Salus infirmorum,	Health of the weak,
Refugium peccatorum,	Refuge of sinners,
Consolatrix afflictorum,	Comforter of the afflicted,

Ora pro nobis.

Pray for us.

Auxilium Christianorum,	Help of Christians,
Regina angelorum,	Queen of angels,
Regina patriarcharum,	Queen of patriarchs,
Regina prophetarum,	Queen of prophets,
Regina apostolorum,	Queen of apostles,
Regina martyrum,	Queen of martyrs,
Regina confessorum,	Queen of confessors,
Regina virginum,	Queen of virgins,
Regina sanctorum omnium,	Queen of all saints,
Regina sine labe originali concepta,	Queen conceived without original sin,

Ora Pro nobis. / *Pray for us.*

Agnus Dei, qui tollis peccata mundi, *parce nobis Domine.*

Lamb of God, who takest away the sins of the world, *Spare us, O Lord.*

Agnus Dei, qui tollis peccata mundi,

Lamb of God, who takest away the sins of the world,

Exaudi nos, Domine.

Graciously hear us, O Lord.

Agnus Dei, qui tollis peccata mundi,

Lamb of God who takest away the sins of the world,

Miserere nobis.

Have mercy on us.

V. Ora pro nobis sancta Dei Genitrix.

R. Ut digni efficiamur promissionibus Christi.

Oremus.

Defende, quæsumus, Domine, beata Maria semper virgine, intercedente, istam ab omni adversitate familiam : et toto corde tibi prostratam ab hostium propitius tuere clementer insidiis. Per Christum Dominum nostrum. Amen.

R. Amen.

Hymnus.

Tantum ergo sacramentum,
Veneremur, cernui ;

Et antiquum documentum,
Novo cedat ritui :

V. Pray for us, O holy Mother of God.

R. That we may be made worthy of the promises of Christ.

Let us pray.

Defend, O Lord, we beseech thee, by the intercession of blessed Mary ever virgin, this thy family from all adversity; and mercifully protect us, who prostrate ourselves before thee with all our hearts, from the snares of the enemy. Through Christ our Lord. Amen. *R.* Amen.

Hymn.

To this mysterious table now,
Our knees, our hearts, and sense we bow:
Let ancient rites resign their place
To nobler elements of grace :

Præstet fides supplementum,
Sensuum defectui.

And faith for all defects supply,
While sense is lost in mystery.

Genitori, genitoque,

To God the Father born of none,

Laus et jubilatio :

To Christ His co-eternal Son,

Salus, honor, virtus quoque,
Sit et benedictio :

And Holy Ghost, whose equal rays
From both proceed, be equal praise :

Procedenti ab utroque,
Compar sit laudatio. Amen.

One honour, jubilee, and fame,
For ever bless his glorious name. Amen.

V. Panem de cœlo præstitisti eis.

V. Thou gavest them bread from heaven,

R. Omne delectamentum in se habentem.

R. Having in it all that is delicious.

Oremus.

Let us Pray.

Deus qui nobis sub sacramento mirabili, passionis tuæ memoriam reliquisti: tribue quæsumus, ita nos corporis et sanguinis tui, sacra

O God, who in this wonderful sacrament hast left us a memorial of thy passion; grant us, we beseech thee, so to reverence the sacred mysteries

mysteria venerari, ut redemptionis tui fructum in nobis jugiter sentiamus. Qui vivis et regnas in sæcula sæculorum. Amen.

Adoremus in æternum,

Sanctissimum Sacramentum.

of thy body and blood, as in our souls to be always sensible of the redemption thou hast purchased for us. Who livest, &c. Amen.

O Sacrament most holy, O Sacrament divine,

All praise and all thanksgiving be every moment thine.

Psalm cxvi.

Laudate Dominum omnes gentes: *laudate eum omnes populi.

Quoniam confirmata est super nos misericordia ejus: * et veritas Domini manet in æternum.

Gloria Patri, et Filio, * et Spiritui Sancto.

Sicut erat in principio, et nunc, et semper, * et in sæcula sæculorum. Amen.

Psalm cxvi.

O praise the Lord, all ye nations: praise him, all ye people.

For his mercy is confirmed upon us: and the truth of the Lord remaineth for ever.

Glory be to the Father, and to the Son, and to the Holy Ghost·

As it was in the beginning, is now, and ever shall be, world without end. Amen.

Adoremus in æter-
num,
  Sanctissimum Sa-
cramentum.

O Sacrament most holy,
O Sacrament divine,

All praise and all thanksgiving be every moment
thine.

INDEX.